A Diary of Daeda's Wood

General Editor
Sylvie Nickels

Production Editor
Mary Robinson

Daeda's Wood celebrates its tenth
birthday in 2006. We think it's a model story
of what can happen when a major charity
co-operates with a local community

Between us we changed the map just a little,
revitalised our local environment,
and left a legacy for future generations

Friends of Daeda's Wood

First published 2006 by the Friends of Daeda's Wood

ISBN 10-digit: 0-9552517-0-2
13-digit: 978-0-9552517-0-2

Design and production: Photoscript, Deddington, Oxon

Printed and bound in the United Kingdom by Antony Rowe Ltd, 2 Whittle Drive
Highfield Industrial Estate, Eastbourne, East Sussex BN23 6QT, England

Contents

To Henri Biolley (p. 2)
who would have been amused by Daeda's Wood
— and loved it

Maps and Access

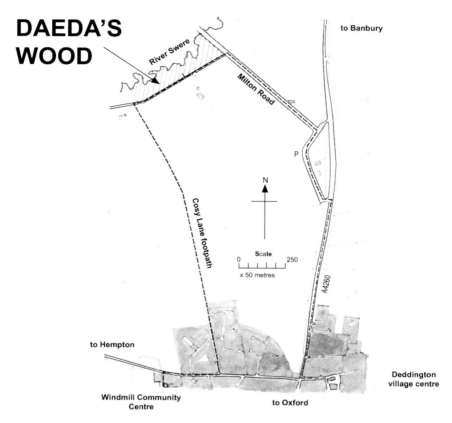

DAEDA'S WOOD

River Swere

to Banbury

Milton Road

P

N

Scale

0   250

x 50 metres

Cosy Lane footpath

A4260

to Hempton

Deddington village centre

Windmill Community Centre

to Oxford

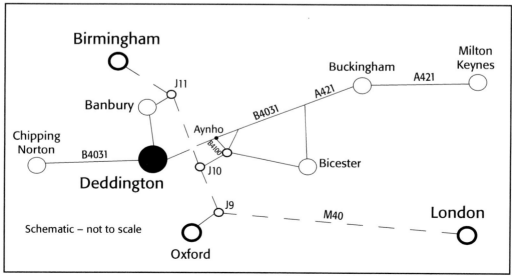

Birmingham

J11

Banbury

Chipping Norton

B4031

Deddington

Aynho

B4100

J10

J9

Oxford

B4031

A421

Buckingham

A421

Milton Keynes

Bicester

M40

London

Schematic – not to scale

1996

Returning jet-lagged from Australia in late November 1995, I find a message on my answering machine. 'We're the Woodland Trust', it says, more or less, 'and we're hoping to create a wood somewhere near you. Please call us.'

It transpires the Trust is launching a Woods on your Doorstep project by which it aims to create 200 new community woods for the Millennium. A stretch of land bordering the River Swere has become available in our parish. It could become the very first of the Woods on your Doorstep.

The Trust contacts me because, at that time, I am editing our village magazine, the *Deddington News*. They do not know I am already a member of the Woodland Trust. They cannot know that I have a thing about trees because my grandfather, Henri Biolley, was a Swiss forester of repute; he devoted his working life to the study and practice of naturally regenerated forests, as opposed to those planted in serried rows. Unwittingly the Woodland Trust has scored a bull's eye.

Convincing me is the easy bit. Convincing our parish that we should raise £9,000 to buy the land in a considerable hurry is a very different ballgame.

The Parish Council say they will think about it. Public meetings are called. The site is too far, judge some (it is 1.5km from the village centre); too wet, say others; too

Imagine a wood on your doorstep - by the year 2000!

Deddington has the opportunity to be the **FIRST COMMUNITY** in the country to benefit from the Woodland Trust's exciting 'Woods on your Doorstep' project to create new woods on the edge of towns and villages to celebrate the new Millennium.

The Woodland Trust has made an offer for 9.5 acres at Bloxham Bridge on the southern bank of the River Swere and connected to Deddington both by the road to Milton and the bridleway towards Deddington Mill.

We need local people to help us raise the money to buy the land and create the new wood - **our initial target is £9,000.** If we raise this amount, the National Lottery (Millennium Commission) will back the project - **they will match the money,** so we can **DOUBLE EVERY POUND** we raise. We are also seeking support from local councils, companies and the Forestry Commission, but we still need your help.

We need your pledge of support NOW to help us purchase this site by the end of January or the opportunity may be lost forever.

You're the key! Don't miss the chance to help us make this happen.

Woods on your Doorstep

URGENT!
WE NEED YOUR HELP TO RAISE £9,000 BY THE END OF JANUARY

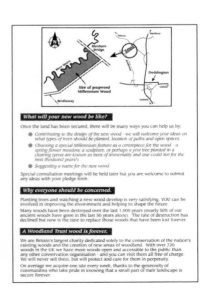

Site of proposed Millennium Wood

What will your new wood be like?

Once the land has been secured, there will be many ways you can help us by:

● Contributing to the design of the new wood - we will welcome your ideas on what types of trees should be planted, location of paths and open spaces.

● Choosing a special Millennium feature as a centrepiece for the wood - a spring flower meadow, a sculpture, or perhaps a yew tree planted in a clearing (yews are known as trees of immortality and one could live for the next thousand years!).

● Suggesting a name for the new wood.

Special consultation meetings will be held later but you are welcome to submit any ideas with your pledge form.

Why everyone should be concerned.

Planting trees and watching a new wood develop is very satisfying. YOU can be involved in improving the environment and helping to shape the future.

Many woods have been destroyed over the last 1,000 years (nearly 50% of our ancient woods have gone in the last 50 years alone). The rate of destruction has declined but now is the time to replace those woods that have been lost forever.

A Woodland Trust wood is forever.

We are Britain's largest charity dedicated solely to the conservation of the nation's existing woods and the creation of new areas of woodland. With over 720 woods in the UK we have more woods open and accessible to the public than any other conservation organisation - and you can visit them all free of charge. We will never sell them, but will protect and care for them in perpetuity.

On average we acquire one site every week, thanks to the generosity of communities who take pride in knowing that a small part of their landscape is secure forever.

expensive, pronounce yet others. Then a voice of sanity is heard: why not forget about ourselves and think of future generations?

The *Deddington News* distribution team does sterling work, delivering a fund-raising appeal through every letterbox in the parish. Our Parish Clerk agrees to make his office the collecting point for any pledges of support. Initially, the trickle seems barely more than a drip, but this is the eve of Christmas and New Year preoccupations. By late February 1996, we have reached £5,000 and the World Wildlife Fund are making encouraging noises. Finally, as we approach the magic £9,000, the Parish Council agree to underwrite the remaining shortfall.

More public meetings while the 4.5-hectare site grows and harvests its last crop of corn. We choose the wood's name, to reflect the Saxon leader from which Deddington itself has derived its name. Jill Butler, the Woodland Officer in charge, asks for our ideas to incorporate into her design (see pp. 22–3) and we settle for a wildflower meadow and a stretch of wheelchair-friendly path.

In October, we mastermind a mini-planting with some of our schoolchildren, to be featured in a BBC countryside programme. Sunday, 24 November is nominated the all-important Community Planting Day for the 3,500 trees waiting to be planted. We awake to gales and driving rain that soon turns to snow.

The weather is diabolical, yet in spite of it over 100 people of all ages and sizes arrive with their spades to dig for Daeda. Watching them at work, heads down against the driving snow, I know our faith in the project has been justified. Between us we plant some hundreds of the trees, the rest to be put in by Woodland Trust contractors in the following days. The Trust also provides a small marquee and supply of hot soup. We make good use of both.

In December Colin Robinson is successful in raising a grant from the Oxfordshire Rural Community Council to support our tree planting and wildflower planting events. Mike Williamson becomes our Treasurer and the Friends of Daeda's Wood is born.

Tree Planting

Staking out the site prior to planting day

Sylvie consults Jill Butler over a box of saplings

Erecting the marquee

November 1996

*Planting day begins
with a steady
drizzle…*

*… and then the drizzle turns
to driving snow*

1997

January: Frost and snow over Daeda's bare expanses. Neat regiments of plastic sheaths mark the 3,500 or so planted 'sticks' that will one day become a wood. Imagination works overtime.

March: A pleasant diversion. The Berkshire, Buckinghamshire and Oxfordshire Naturalists' Trust (now Wildlife Trust: BBOWT) decides to build an otter holt on Daeda's bank of the River Swere in the hope of luring this attractive creature up from the Cherwell Valley. The holt is constructed on a base of logs topped by shaggy brushwood. 'The mink'll take over, mark my words', grunts a local pessimist (and nine years later we are still not sure of the outcome.)

April: Cherwell District Council offer us a stretch of surfaced path for wheelchair users. Engineers come to debate the best composition of the surface. Some riverside willows are pollarded as part of the management cycle which will also include mowing paths and coppicing. Once we have trees, of course.

We hold a community wildflower planting event. The Woodland Trust provides the seeds and plugs of species most suited to the terrain (see pp. 12–13). The earth has been prepared, and we are each given a mixture of seed and sand and told what to do. There is a good turnout and at the end of the day we survey the expanse of brown earth thoughtfully. Imaginations continue to work overtime.

June–September: Someone must have arranged a rain dance – the result a rogue regrowth of previous cereal crops and dormant seeds from a past era. Not least wild oats. We're told that once the trees provide sufficient canopy all this will change. There are a lot of wild flowers, too, but not the ones we planted.

October–November: We have a layby by the main entrance, a stretch of wheelchair-friendly path leading down to the main wildflower meadow, and two seats. Thank you Cherwell District Council. And as it reaches its first birthday, 90 per cent of Daeda's original saplings survive and thrive.

Our plastic sheaths begin to grow …

…but spring rain brings a flourish of rogue regrowth

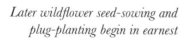

Later wildflower seed-sowing and plug-planting begin in earnest

The wheelchair-friendly path takes graphic shape

The Trees

Hawthorn

Pendunculate oak

The species of trees chosen for the planting areas are typical of lowland riverside woodland. They are a mixture of broad-leaves trees and shrubs comprising: 35 per cent ash; 5 per cent crack willow; 25 per cent oak; 5 per cent almond willow; 5 per cent white willow; 5 per cent goat willow; 3 per cent alder; 5 per cent grey poplar; 1 per cent black poplar; 1 per cent aspen; 3 per cent osier; 2 per cent purple willow; 2 per cent hawthorn; 2 per cent blackthorn; 1 per cent Guelder rose. A few oak seedlings grown from seed from ancient oaks in Windsor Great Park have been planted.

The trees have been planted to achieve an average 3m x 3m spacing; however this means there are variable densities of planting across the site of between 1.5m x 1.5m to 5m x 5m spacing. The shrubs have been planted at 3m x 3m spacing, except in some areas

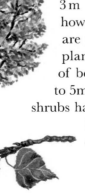

Black poplar

Blackthorn

Alder

where it is necessary to create a more dense barrier to discourage access such as against the planting block to the north west of the site.

There is an area of dense planting in the north west corner of the site to discourage access to the riverbank and meanders.

An otter holt has been installed by the BBOWT Otter Habitation Project using pollarded limbs from an adjacent willow and blackthorn planting across the meander neck to provide a longer-term barrier to access.

Aspen

To create south-facing woodland edge habitat, shrubs have been planted on the southern side of blocks of woodland.

In addition some of the woodland edges will be coppiced on a short rotation (6–8 years) to decrease the gradients of the edges of the woodland blocks to allow sunlight at all times of the year into the rides and wildflower area.

Crack willow

Guelder rose

Ash

For a complete list of trees, see p. 41

1998

February–March: We launch our ongoing mobile exhibition showing, through photos, text and diagrams, how Daeda's Wood has evolved from a barley field. Colin Robinson does marvels enlarging, scanning and mounting the photographs; I write the text, and Jackie and Mike Williamson get the loan of some display boards. It makes its debut in the primary school where, we are told, it attracts a lot of attention.

April: We launch into cyberspace via Deddington OnLine, a village website run by a group of local computing enthusiasts: «http://www.deddington.org.uk/community/daedaswood.html».

Summer: One or two horse riders seem unable to comprehend the notice at either entrance stating there is no bridleway through the wood. A pity. By the end of the year we are obliged to build a squeezegate at one entrance.

In June Bill Drake becomes o/c damselflies, monitoring the two species (Beautiful and Banded – *Calopteryx splendens* and *Calopteryx virgo)* for which the Swere at this point apparently provides an ideal breeding ground. It's important that this should not become shaded out by too many trees.

Dock is rampant and needs treating, but there are signs that last year's spring wildflower sowing was not in vain: in particular ox-eye daisy, plantain and yarrow, and we are hopeful of ragged robin.

On a June day I suddenly become aware of a small flock of blue tits flying from tree to tree. 'Hey, here's a wood', I hear them say. A seminal moment.

The Environment Authority (formerly Rivers Authority) arrive for their periodical clean-up, including a mass pollarding of riverside willows to forestall possible river blockage. It leaves a bit of a mess but plenty of new deadwood habitat.

In July, much of the county – in the form of parish councillors, conservationists, farmers, ramblers – foregather at Deddington's Windmill Centre for a Countryside Forum arranged by the Cherwell District Council, with a presentation by Woodland Trust Officer Jill Butler. After the Forum, we troop down to Daeda's under blue black clouds, are treated to a fantastic double rainbow and a mainly sunlit return. 'How do you get a wood like this?', someone asks enviously. I refer them to Jill Butler.

October: An Environmental Extravaganza at the Windmill Centre brings over a dozen conservation organisations to display imaginative schemes for conserving and encouraging various aspects of our environment – and nearly 1,000 visitors from all over the county. Several ask, 'how do we get a wood like yours?'.

Dramatic skies greet the walkers at Daeda's Wood

Participants in CDC's Countryside Forum on the way down Cosy Lane towards Daeda's Wood

A seat, a path, and a wood beginning to grow

Some of the 'Friends' at the Countryside Forum display at the Windmill Community Centre

'Look, that's me!', children from Deddington Primary School

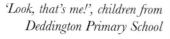

Daeda's Flora

We only began a formal annual check of the Daeda's Wood flora in 2002. Before that I and others had noted the prevailing indigenous plants – meadow cranesbill, plantain, teasel, greater willow herb, etc. – and monitored the progress of those introduced during the official wild flower planting, of which ox-eye daisy, ragged robin and meadowsweet are the most graceful and eye-catching. And I must stress that we are not trained botanists. Dithering over identification is not unknown. We stand in the wood, turning the pages of our *Guide to British Wild Flowers*. Is this creeping thistle (*Cirsium arvense*) or marsh thistle (*Cirsium palustre*)? Does this St John's wort look 'hairy' or 'square-stalked' to you? In our defence, we have tried to ensure that the annual flora lists contain only the names of verified species. Walter Meagher has given invaluable support here.

The range of wild flowers is remarkable. Most are indigenous. Some, soil specific, were suggested by the Woodland Trust and planted either as seed or plugs in 1997 or October 2000. Some plants stay put, others swan around. Banks of the beautiful purple tufted vetch appear by the Swere one year. Next year the vetches do a flit and colonise the far side of the central path. Why? Are they economic migrants (fairer conditions) or just footloose?

Other plants appear 'For One Night Only'. Two springs ago I found clumps of white violet at the north west corner of the boundary hedge. No sign since. Again, why? In 2004 the Meaghers led us to a flourishing nettle-leaved bellflower, an interesting arrival. In 2005 sadly it has shut up shop. The changing tree canopy and related ground cover density may influence this floral rise and fall. The little wild pansy has largely disappeared as the leaf canopy has thickened or, in open spaces, cleavers, thistles and tufted grasses have gained a hold. The reverse also happens. Cowslips, at first sparse, are now well established. Musk mallow and primroses have arrived in the wild flower meadow.

We are fortunate too in the aquatic plants in this short stretch of the Swere. Yellow water-lilies cover the surface in summer, vying for space with the upstanding arrowheads.

Then there are the incomers – pushy and determined to be noticed. Gardeners (?) have dumped their waste in a corner of the wood just before the Swere bridge. Come February and March the corner is now a suburban garden – snowdrops, daffodils, exotically-tinged comfrey, purple crocus. We allow them list space, firmly designating them 'garden escapees'. Johnny-come-latelys must know their place. Impossible to mention all the plants. Best of all, go down to the wood and see the seasonal magic for yourself.

KRISTIN THOMPSON

Ragged robin

Cuckoo flower

For a complete flora
list, see p. 41

Meadow cranesbill

Musk mallow

1999

Sadly, 'our' Woodland Officer, Jill Butler, moves on to higher things, but first introduces us to her pleasant successor Ian Gray. And, due to ill health, Bill Drake has to give up on monitoring damselflies, a responsibility taken over by Sue Goddard.

March: A walk along Daeda's bank of the Swere with Walter Meagher is eye-opening. I hadn't realised there were so many elm suckers, none of which, alas, will survive beyond a certain young age before succumbing to Dutch elm disease. A study of the crack willows and the way they host other species in their 'cracks' – especially ash and sycamore – is fascinating.

May: Lord and Lady Sainsbury of Preston Candover look in on us – indeed do a leisurely one-hour circuit of this first of the Woods on your Doorstep scheme to which the Sainsbury Family Charitable Trusts have provided considerable financial support. The wood is looking a treat: a mass of willow catkins, and the black poplar, alder, hawthorn and guelder rose all satisfyingly green.

And Daeda's Wood is now literally on the map as the Cherwell District Council's Deddington Circular Walk, which passes through it, is inaugurated.

By the end of the month the wildflower meadow is a magnificent tangle of ragged robin, buttercup and ox-eye daisy; and looking across from almost anywhere there is truly the sense of a woodland in the making.

Summer: There is developing contention over dog faeces: some dog owners apparently cannot comprehend that many of us do not appreciate these gratuitous additions to the wood. The Woodland Trust, somewhat surprised to find themselves faced with this kind of site management, agree to the installation of a dog poo bin, funded by the Parish Council, on condition that it is emptied regularly.

Many people comment on how close the trees are planted to each other. In fact the distance is the maximum set down by the Forest Authority, but it also serves to encourage the more rapid development of a canopy and, in turn, discourage rank growth at ground level.

The wildflower meadow, after its moments of spring glory, develops a distinctly tangled look, but the creamy expanses of yarrow, interspersed with blue self-heal and purple knapweed along sections of the main ride, are a joy to see.

The grass rides are cut several times a year

Lord and Lady Sainsbury (centre) drop in on Daeda's Wood

Yarrow and self-heal along the main ride

Daeda's Wood gets on the map as the Deddington Circular Walk becomes a reality

Daeda's Butterflies ...

A s a very small child I was taught to identify and appreciate butterflies. My qualifications for monitoring their presence in Daeda's Wood amount to no more than that. For the past three years, twice a month from May to September, I've walked the wood, listing whatever butterflies were feeding or on the wing at the time. The weather is all-important. Butterflies prefer sunny still conditions. On cloudy or windy days they sulk in their lepidopteran tents.

The most common butterflies in the wood, appearing all through the summer, are the large and small whites, their floppy flight unmistakable. Meadow browns and speckled woods are also frequent fliers. Orange tips and brimstones venture out in May and you can see the occasional red admiral flying along the open rides. By June, the small tortoiseshell is commonplace and small blues, male and female (the female not so blue), are hovering over the grasses.

July, depending on the weather and the plant growth, can be bonanza time. The wood's creeping thistle, so disliked by dog walkers and ramblers, is the peacock's idea of heaven. Dozens of them descend to feed, then lazily circle and return to settle on the next purple flower. The colours are jewel-like. It's a breathtaking sight. Painted ladies too, enjoy the thistles and commas, with their beautiful shape, open and shut their wings in the sunlight. I have twice seen the marbled white in July, not rare but uncommon enough to make me glad of confirmation of their presence in the Swere valley in Walter Meagher and Peter Sheasby's book, *Portrait of a River* (2005). Also seen in July, large numbers

Peacock

Marbled white

of common blue and skippers which, alas, I'm too ignorant to differentiate.

By chance, the August butterfly tally in the wood has been disappointing. I chose the wrong day, or the sky clouded over and only the regulars like the whites, tortoiseshells and meadow browns were on the wing. Subsequent years may give a different picture of this month.

September sees a diminution of numbers, but red admirals, peacocks, small coppers and speckled woods are still flying and feeding.

KRISTIN THOMPSON

Common blue

For a list of Lepidoptera (2003–05), see p. 30

... and Damselflies

In 1997 the Woodland Trust Officer suggested that there should be an annual survey of the damselfly population in Daeda's Wood. There was local concern that the two species, beautiful demoiselle (*Calopteryx virgo*) and banded demoiselle (*Calopteryx splendens*), both of which had been recorded on the site, might be affected by the future growth of the trees overhanging the River Swere. Since then, this survey has been carried out annually, first by Bill Drake and then by me and Nancy White who joined me later.

Banded demoiselle

A typical season for damselflies runs from mid-May to mid-August. They prefer warm sunny weather with not too much wind. We try to make a weekly visit, depending on the weather, each time working from east to west close to the river bank, recording – sometimes with difficulty – the number of damselflies on the wing. We keep records of the numbers seen on each visit. These vary a lot but are at their peak during June and July. At the end of the season the results are sent to the Woodland Trust which prepares and keeps graphs of the totals.

These beautiful insects with their brilliantly coloured wings are discussed and illustrated in *Portrait of a River*. In spite of the increasing density of the wood and, recently, the more frequent appearance of the predatory dragonflies, the damselfly population appears to be fairly stable. This is very encouraging news for us all.

SUE GODDARD AND NANCY WHITE

2000

The new Millennium brings several highlights.

February: Most of the world descends upon us in the form of forestry students from ten countries across four continents. They come with their tutor from the Oxford Institute of Forestry to discuss the significance of a community woodland. It is the day after the dog poo bin is installed. The lady from the Cameroons is much amused by this.

We also find we have a phantom pruner; someone has taken a pair of secateurs to a number of trees – effectively but uninvited.

Spring: We trace the phantom pruner, a well-wisher whose intentions are of the best – merely misplaced. Our display goes up in the entrance hall of Deddington Primary School. And among the energetic Friends of Daeda's Wood the pace hots up as 4 June and the Millennium Family Picnic approach.

4 June: Take a day of sun and breeze and scudding clouds; add about a hundred people, nearly half of them children; mix in cheerful voices and whoops of laughter as muscles strain at the tug-of-war; sprinkle with earnest frowns of concentration on the scent of 16 treasure hunt clues (*see panel*); stir the whole with sturdy young trees and a multi-coloured tangle of wild flowers – and there, more or less, you have the Millennium Family Picnic. Not the whisper of a radio, no one sneaking the wild flowers and, afterwards, not a scrap of litter. Magic.

Someone asks me where to get dog litter bags. I tell them that most people find the supermarket plastic variety effective.

Autumn: The wood seems suddenly to have 'taken off'. Someone even claims to have got lost in it, and it is true that, with the trees in full foliage, you can no longer see across it. Kristin and I do a botanical tour and come up with the best list so far. In October we have another flower-planting event financed by a generous donor, aiming to increase the spread of wild flowers. An age range of 20 months to four-score years turn out with wellies and trowels to plant about 600 plugs.

There is still trouble with dog faeces.

December: The name of Daeda's Wood echoes round the Halls of Westminster. The occasion is a reception in the Members' Dining Room of the House of Commons, hosted by Paddy Tipping, MP, for that other little wood, Sherwood Forest. It is to celebrate the achievement of the Woodland Trust's goal of 200 new woods for the Millennium (see pp. 42–3). The Woodland Trust bigwigs are out in full force, and an impressive number of MPs, as well as a lot of we 'little people' who beaver away in our corners. As the first of the Woods on your Doorstep, Daeda's Wood gets several honourable mentions, as do the Friends of Daeda's Wood, as a shining example of community commitment. I am asked a lot of questions about how we operate and, as I list our achievements, I realise what a great group we are. And preen on behalf of us all.

The Treasure Hunt

The first picnic we plan is to celebrate the Millennium. A treasure hunt is apparently mandatory. At an early committee meeting it is decided that the clues shall be in rhyme, so I volunteer because I like rhyming. Kristin offers to help me and we produce our first set of clues.

'Too hard', groan one half of the committee.

'Too easy', laugh the other half.

We persevere, keeping to a theme: anything that can be found in the wood.

Practicalities take over, such as where and how to place the clues, how to prevent 'cheating', what prizes to give. We write 16 clues, each suggesting something to be seen in a wood. Each also bears one letter of a mystery word which will eventually form an anagram which has to be solved as well. For prizes we give identification books on flowers, trees, birds, etc.

Johnson's, our local timber yard makes us some stout 3ft posts. We hammer them into thick undergrowth, partly hidden, and pin on the numbered clues inside plastic bags. We add posts for rubbish bags. Just before the event we have a cleaning-up-after-dogs meeting and put warning notices along the river bank, although these days the spectacular meanders of the river are very visible through our little trees.

That first picnic goes brilliantly. The clues are still considered too hard and too easy but everyone has fun. My favourite clue? It is No. 16: 'You'll want to squidge/the ubiquitous ? ' (the answer rhymes with squidge).

Conditions are different for our Jubilee treasure hunt two years later. The wood has grown secretive. Competitors cannot see through the leaf screen. We actually keep losing ourselves while we are setting it up again. But although the wood has changed, our theme has not, and the event is as successful as ever.

My favourite clue that year is: 'Good luck if you find four leaves on this plant/ But mostly, when counted, four leaves there aren't'.

We're planning another picnic and I hope I'm asked to rhyme again.

MOLLY NEILD

2000

Overseas students of forestry visit the wood in February

The Millennium Picnic

In Pictures

*And in autumn, more
flower planting*

Designing the Wood

Involving the people of Deddington in the design of their new woodland was crucial for Daeda's Wood, the first of the Woodland Trust's proposed 200 Woods on your Doorstep to be created for the 2000 Millennium. And local people did respond enthusiastically through questionnaire replies, public meetings and by helping to plant the trees and wildflower meadow for themselves.

The Woodland Trust believes that new woodland is vital to improve our quality of life – to visit and enjoy a healthy walk, to provide important refuges for wildlife and to add texture to our beautiful landscape. The design of a new wood must achieve all of these and more.

Daeda's Wood is very easy to reach on foot or bike via a scenic bridlepath from Deddington or by car from the Deddington to Milton road (p. 1). Although a relatively small wood, a figure of eight path network was built into the design to allow visitors to appreciate many of the key features of a rapidly changing and emerging wood land – the variety of British broadleaved trees and shrubs, sunny woodland edges, the existing hedgerows and especially access to the banks of the meandering River Swere. A path to the heart of the wood from the main entrance was surfaced so that as many people as possible could enjoy it with the minimum of difficulty.

The choice of trees and shrubs can make a lot of difference to wildlife

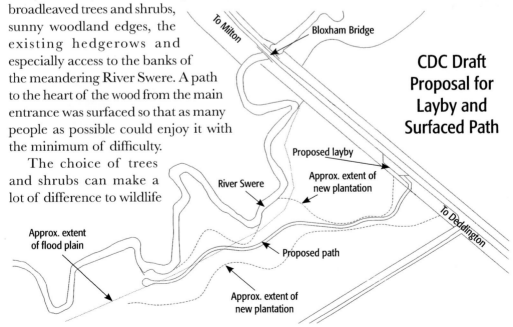

To Milton

Bloxham Bridge

CDC Draft Proposal for Layby and Surfaced Path

Proposed layby

Approx. extent of new plantation

River Swere

To Deddington

Approx. extent of flood plain

Proposed path

Approx. extent of new plantation

and to the landscape. Woodland is one of our richest habitats and a good mix will provide the varied structure and sustainable food supplies throughout the year that will benefit a wide variety of plants and animals. Following discussion with local people, 15 different species of tree and shrubs were chosen to suit the ground conditions in Daeda's Wood and to fit in with the surrounding landscape. Black poplar, which is one of the UK's rarest trees, was included as it is found quite frequently in the area around Deddington and is characteristic of river valleys. Special attention was given to the strategic location of flowering shrubs along south facing rides and the woodland edge to ensure they benefit from sunny positions to provide valuable flower pollen and nectar sources.

As a Millennium feature, a part of every Wood on your Doorstep, Deddington people chose to create a wildflower meadow in the heart of the area. Once again species were chosen that like damp conditions such as the beautiful ragged robin and will provide nectar sources for butterflies, damselflies and other insects.

Views of the wood from different vantage points around it are always taken into consideration, as well as views to the outside from inside the wood. Daeda's Wood is beautifully situated in the valley of the River Swere and visible from a long way away. As the trees grow it is hoped that they will enhance the landscape of this lovely river valley. Equally it is the intention to keep glimpses of the surrounding landscape from different spots inside the wood to make a visit more interesting at any time of the year.

JILL BUTLER

Map of Daeda's Wood on original information board at the wood's entrance

23

2001

S **pring:** In March we return from a long absence abroad to find the countryside under siege from foot and mouth disease. The wood, along with much else, remains closed until mid-May.

The April *Deddington News* carries an excellent survey of our local farmers' views on the foot and month crisis. Livestock cannot be moved, disinfecting is the order of the day, footpaths are closed, farmers' families venture off their land in disinfected clothing if they venture at all, many incomes plummet. All farmers express their appreciation for the support and thoughtfulness shown by so many people – except those who tear down the notices advising that rights of way are closed. Our own closure notice on the entrance gate is removed several times. 'Where are the animals?' someone scrawls in chalk on the gatepost. They presumably have not heard of the muntjacs who respect no boundaries and are known to be enjoying the rare undisturbed calm of the wood.

Summer: In general the wood seems to have enjoyed the rest. It has acquired a wilder, tawnier feel, and there is more of everything: more wild flowers, more butterflies and damselflies, more birds and, of course, bigger and better trees.

We also have a new Woodland Officer, John Brown.

December: There are signs of horse riding through the wood, so our 'No Bridlepath' signs go up again; and someone has vandalised the dog poo bin. Pity about people. But, in all its natural aspects, the wood thrives. Some walkers have complained about the increasingly rampant creeping thistle. John Brown points out that this provides excellent habitat for insects and food for birds. I find myself wondering for whom the wood is really designed. No doubt we'll find a compromise as usual.

WOODLAND TRUST **WOOD OPEN**

Following an assessment of the risk of spreading Foot & Mouth Disease, this site has now been re-opened for you to walk in.

PLEASE follow this code to avoid endangering farm animals and people's livelihoods:

- **Obey official signs.**
- **Respect and follow instructions from farmers and other land managers.**
- **Keep dogs on a short lead at all times.**
- **Clean your boots between visits**
- **Do not touch or feed farm animals.**
- **Do not enter fields with farm animals**
- **Do not enter farm yards**
- **Do not leave waste or scraps of food or litter.**
- **Do not park your car in areas where farm animals gather such as field gateways.**

The Code is based on expert advice from the Ministry of Agriculture and Fisheries and Food

The Woodland Trust, Autumn Park, Dysart Road, Grantham, Lincolnshire, NG31 6LL. Telephone: 01476 581111. Registered Charity No.294344

Keeping Woodland Alive

Foot and mouth disease closes Daeda's Wood, to the disapproval of some

The wood adopts a wilder feel after its rest

Foot and Mouth Disease in the UK

Foot and Mouth is a non-fatal, viral, highly infectious disease of cloven hoofed animals. It is a notifiable disease and there is at present no known cure. Although vaccination is used as a preventive measure in other parts of the world, it is not allowed in the UK as the relevant authorities consider the slaughter of all infected and contact animals to be the best method of control. The symptoms are sudden and acute: lameness, loss of body condition, sharp fall in milk production, abortion in breeding stock, and blisters in the foot and in the mouth areas.

The virus is spread via direct contact between animals, through animal feeds, and it is also carried on the wind, by birds and wild animals, human clothing and vehicle tyres.

There have been a number of outbreaks since the first in 1839, and in 1884 the compulsory slaughter and compensation act became law. To date all outbreaks in this country have been due to the import of infected animals, meat and meat products. This year's was caused by feeding imported food waste to pigs (a practice now banned) and resulted in the slaughter of nine million animals.

Although compensation is paid for all animals slaughtered, no account is taken of the loss of income or the cost of restocking. On a wider front many small businesses suffer uncompensated loss due to the closure of large areas of countryside.

GEORGE FENEMORE

Birds and Animals

My sketchy amateur notes from earliest visits, even pre-planting, were peppered with references to hyperactive flocks of yellowhammers and tree sparrows. This was, after all, good arable land, habitat of choice for such species. In the winter, visiting Scandinavian members of the thrush family, especially fieldfare, collected noisily in the taller trees along the Swere.

And that first post-planting Christmas morning, a magical azure flash announced a kingfisher hunting the Swere. Obligingly it paused to preen and be admired.

I have noted a rather surprising number of water birds. Mallards are regularly flushed in twos or threes. The odd moorhen has stalked laconically across Fred Lovell's fields, across the river. Several times I have caught a grey heron on lift-off, no doubt disturbed by my presence. Once I startled a pair of snipe, and would have doubted my own eyes if their zig-zag flight were not unmistakeable.

Then the summer visitors found us. First on my list was the blackcap, its fluid song making up for its infuriating invisibility. The unbeautiful but unmistakeable chiffchaff call of the chiffchaff is usually a little distant since it prefers trees taller than Daeda could offer until very recently. But the very similar willow warbler is very content, thank you, with our profusion of foliage through which it moves restlessly, pausing briefly to announce its territory with its plaintive little song. In recent summers I have also been aware of the regular presence of whitethroats.

The green woodpecker's cackle has long been a regular sound, and there are less frequent glimpses of great spotted woodpecker working its way through a tree. I have yet to see either nuthatch or treecreeper but have no doubt they are there.

From time to time you see a hovering kestrel or glimpse a hunting sparrowhawk, but you have to look into more distant heights for the broad-winged glide of a buzzard riding the thermals. I am told hobby has been seen, but I'm still looking.

Daeda's fauna is dominated by the rabbit against which every sapling has been protected since day one by a plastic guard. As they grew, the trees mostly burst out of their guards which over a period have been collected and bagged by our well-wishers, not least the Deddington Boys Brigade.

Muntjac have been seen and once I encountered a fox. It came strolling out of one of the rides, paused to assess me and then strolled away, unhurried, through the trees. I know this is an absurd anthropomorphism, but I interpreted this as mutual recognition of the right of each of us to be there.

SYLVIE NICKELS

Work begins on the otter holt

... and the completed structure

Daeda's Bats

All of our 16 species of bats use woodland, woodland edge or rides to forage for their insect prey and the majority of them have evolved to use trees for their summer and winter roosts. Their numbers have declined drastically in Britain in recent years.

The location of Daeda's Wood increases its importance for bats. Continuous treelines and hedgerows provide connectivity of the landscape, which is important for commuting between foraging sites. Watercourses provide excellent feeding grounds, water to drink and the bankside vegetation provides habitats for insect prey and valuable cover whilst foraging. The woodland is sheltered, thus providing different microclimates for insects and bats. The more intensively managed area surrounding the wood may have large numbers of insects but fewer species which could lead to food shortages for bats at certain times of year.

In time, the trees will develop rot holes, cracks and crevices, loose bark and eventually holes produced by woodpeckers, all of which provide roost sites for bats. Trees are used as roosts because they meet varying needs at different times of the year. For example, in spring and early summer breeding females cluster together to retain body heat and further conserve energy by selecting sites in sheltered trees which receive sunshine for part of the day, or by using a small hole surrounded by thick wood which provides insulation.

On warm, calm summer evenings bats may be seen flying above the trees searching for food. In recent years very limited bat detector surveys have produced records of Pipistrelle (*Pipistrellus spp.*) feeding in the wood and Daubenton's (*Myotis daubentonii*) feeding along the river.

L.R. TIPPING
(Oxfordshire Bat Group)

2002

Daeda's Wood joins the growing list of venues for events to celebrate the Queen's Jubilee. We settle for 23 June, thus avoiding the events-packed Jubilee weekend itself (1–4 June). We plan a programme similar to the one for the Millennium with Molly in charge of the Treasure Hunt (p. 19), and our hard-working team rolls up its collective sleeves. Alas, we are losing Jackie and Mike Williamson to Wales, but they are available to o/c the tug-of-war arrangements before they go.

Spring: John Brown, currently Our Man at the Woodland Trust, warns that a prominent mature sycamore pollard on the wood's southern boundary will need drastic further pollarding in the interests of safety. Sizeable branches that have fallen into the Swere in the teeth of recent gales are also due for removal.

Our display, now celebrating Daeda's first five years, goes up in the primary school entrance hall and, in April, moves to the library.

Summer: John Craven, presenter of BBC One's *Countryfile* programme, agrees to judge our Jubilee Treasure Hunt and present the prizes. Between 80 and 100 converge on Daeda for the Family Picnic, armed with blankets, collapsible seats, coolers and picnic baskets, sun brollies and sun cream. And, yes, they do actually need the latter for the sun shines upon us throughout most of the proceedings.

It's a joy to hear the whoops of excitement as tiny muscles take the strain in a series of tugs-of-war – and some not-so-tiny muscles as well. And to see those of all sizes in earnest search of the Treasure Hunt clues.

It's also a pleasure to have with us Jill Butler, who held Daeda's hand, as it were, from the wood's inception and was responsible for its design and composition (pp. 22–3); and John Brown. He tells us that the much-abominated creeping thistle will take time to clear as cutting is pointless for this species which propagates through underground shoots. We remain confident he will find a solution.

Autumn: The best flora list year (see p. 41). We move our display to the Parish Church. A mystery 'heritage tree' post appears near the lower seat by the wildflower meadow. Investigation reveals it is part of a 'Sponsor a Heritage Tree' fund-raising promotion by the Woodland Trust. Some of us would have like to be consulted before the post went up, but we are pleased that we qualify: in this case, with a veteran willow pollard.

In October we organise a working party to clean up the layby and nearby hedges. The developing wood's autumn colours are especially satisfying this year.

*John Craven presenting the
Treasure Hunt prize to
Freddie Meagher*

*The
Jubilee
Picnic*

2003

January: After heavy rain the Swere overspills its banks. The trees – mainly ash – rising out of their own reflections make an attractive picture in the winter sunlight. The main path is exceedingly soggy and, from all the signs, must have spawned an army of muddy paws.

Spring: John Brown confirms that chemical treatment of the creeping thistle is out of the question because of the potential harm to the wild flowers. He promises that the developing canopy will shade it out under the trees and, in due course, vigorous cutting will discourage it elsewhere.

Summer: We are away in a hot, dry place (Utah) all summer, but your summer here competes in heat and aridity. Kristin reports a colourful wildflower meadow and begins to monitor the butterflies (see panel below) which apparently appreciate the creeping thistle even if no one else does. Sue and Nancy register a good damselfly summer. What is forcing well-defined tracks through the dense barriers of goosegrass and nettle? asks Kristin. Is it muntjac, badger, fox or just the domestic dog? I'll take a bet on the d.d.

Autumn: On our return from Utah I manage to lose my way on my first visit to the wood. Evasive tactics round bramble and thistle eventually bring me whence I began

---

LIST OF LEPIDOPTERA 2003–05*

Admiral, red, *Vanessa atalanta*
Blue, common, *Polyommatus icarus*
Brimstone, *Gonepteryx rhamni*
Brown, meadow, *Maniloa jurtina*
Comma, *Polygonia c-album*
Copper, small, *Lycaena phlaeas*
Orange tip, *Anthocharis cardamines*
Painted lady, *Cynthia cardui*

Peacock, *Inachis io*
Skipper, large, *Ochlodes venatus*
Speckled wood, *Pararge aegeria*
Tortoiseshell, small, *Aglais urticae*
White, large, *Pieris brassicae*
White, marbled, *Melanargia galathea*
White, small, *Pieris rapae*

* The lists contain other tentative sightings, including several members of the blue, brown and skipper families, but unless the identification is secure, I have not added it to the formal tally. *K.T.*

– but it does confirm that increased tree cover is discouraging the spread of thistle as predicted by John Brown.

We say regretful farewells to Jackie and Mike Williamson. Mike was our Treasurer, both have been a great support in the organising of picnics, cleaning of the layby, preparation and mounting of our displays, etc. In our absence, the Friends have acquired some new display boards, courtesy of the Woodland Trust. Thank you WT. In November, the display goes up in the Parish Church.

We do a clean-up job on the layby at the main entrance and fill several rubbish bags. Happily the wood itself remains commendably litter-free so we blame casual users of the layby.

After the January rains

The wood is a favourite among dog walkers

The end of a hot, dry summer

Daeda's River

The River Swere swirls past Daeda's Wood without a thought for problems it may cause. It has a natural tendency, as all rivers do, to overspill the banks in flood-tide. One may tolerate this seasonal aberration without resort to management, as usually the waters will subside. But if overspilling is aided by stream blockage – fallen limbs, even whole trees – it is right to call the Environment Agency, who will remove the offending members. One might argue, on the other hand, on behalf of a more proactive approach, for the pruning of weakened and dead limbs, or, in some cases, removing whole trees. But then, in depleting food resources at lower levels of the ecosystem, Daeda's Wood would lose some of its natural richness. Therefore, a proactive approach might be sacrificed to a policy of 'live and let live'.

Too much shade over the river raises another problem, but not one of river management. Before the Norman Conquest the River Swere was deepened and straightened, leaving permanent marks on the river's form, at nine sites to make leats for powering water-wheels. In more recent times, especially in the 1950s, portions of the river in Deddington parish were deepened and straightened to reduce lowland farm-field flooding. The Swere by Daeda's Wood escaped this surgery; it has a natural sinuosity and a varying depth of water, depending on the rate of bank-carving and the swishing and swashing of sediments on the river bottom.

Sycamore, especially toward the western edge of Daeda's Wood, shades the river-bank as much as crack willow – no, it shades it more – but the willow is more likely to lose limbs to the river's swirl; it is therefore the management of this tree that bears the burden of river management. Strength of trees with long secondary growth stems may be restored by pollarding. We know that, on average, a pollarded willow will live longer than one that is unpollarded. A splendid specimen of this kind occurs not far from where Sor (South) Brook joins the Cherwell. But there is disadvantage to pollarding: if too much wood is cut, the kingfisher will lose its perch.

River management includes monitoring water for pollutants, and therefore for in-vertebrate aquatic and fish life; but these are neglected aspects of local studies made independently of the research of the Environment Agency. Where the river passes Daeda's Wood, the water is deeper than where it passes under Adderbury Bridge, and by the wood the bottom is clay while at the bridge it is gravelly. This makes a difference to the lives of caddis-flies and stoneflies which prefer a faster moving shallow stream on a gravelly bottom to the darker deep and somnolent river by the wood. Fish have been seen in the river, but not plentifully; only the constant patrol of the kingfisher in

Old pollards leaning over the Swere

Purple loosestrife

summertime suggests there is a harvest to be made. On the other hand, the deep slow passages of the river favour the rooting of arrow-head (*Sagittaria sagittifolia*), which flowers in no other portion of the river, and of the yellow water-lily (*Nuphar lutea*) which flowers plentifully in summer, a plant that more than any other in Daeda's Wood has a tropical appearance and suggests the lavish floral treats of the Orient.

WALTER L. MEAGHER

The Otter Holt

After decades of persecution in southern Britain, otters suffered a sudden population crash. The last collected local records, provided by Roy Paginton, are of two young otters playing in the Swere, upstream of Deddington Mill, in the spring of 1952.

In the 1990s the local BBOWT, along with other county wildlife trusts, began working to help the otter populations recover. As part of this programme the Cherwell Otter Habitat Project Officer, Annie Masson, liaised with the Woodland Trust to build an artificial otter holt beside the Swere within the new wood. In February 1997, a small group of local Wildlife Trust volunteers, led by Annie, pollarded two willows and used the branches to build a holt. Friends of the wood and interested passers-by joined in the construction. The aim was to provide a secure but temporary lying-up place for any otters and formed part of a network of artificial holts and trees planted to provide cover along the Swere and other tributaries of the river Cherwell .

Now, nine years on, the artificial holts have decayed but alternative lying-up places have taken their place. Bankside vegetation such as bramble and thorn bushes in Daeda's Wood and other sites provide ideal cover for otters.

The fourth national otter survey of England carried out in 2000–02 confirmed the increase in distribution since the first survey in 1977–79. Otters and otter signs are now a regular occurrence in certain parts of the Thames catchment and show hope of some local recovery.

L.R. TIPPING

2004

February: We have a new Woodland Officer, Neil Chamberlain, who is optimistic that the battle against creeping thistle can be won. There will be three cuts of most of the unshaded affected areas (April, June and September) which should sufficiently weaken the growth over a period of 2–3 years. A few areas in any case are being left for the delectation of butterflies (p. 30) and finches.

Neil is to ask the Cherwell District Council to extend the layby at the main entrance. This will improve wheelchair access and reduce the area of churned up grass created by motorists yet to become proficient in three-point turns. It's in place by the end of the year.

Summer: In June the wood has a positively bridal look, wreathed in creamy cascades of hawthorn. This turns out to be prophetic for the following month Daeda's Wood does indeed become the setting for a marriage ceremony: a highly unusual one at that.

Philip and Judy Chard's wedding is a Druidical celebration. About a hundred people foregather by the wildflower meadow, complete with Morris dancers. The ceremony is led by a High Priest, assisted by colourfully dressed representatives of the four points of the compass from whom are invoked the blessings of earth, fire, water and air. Bride and bridegroom look magnificent. It is a hugely happy occasion and when it is over not a scrap of litter mars the scene.

A week later we hold a village walk. Not many people turn out but some of us bring wine and nibbles, and the wild flowers are fantastic. As we enjoy the combination, Philip and Judy Chard stroll through 'celebrating our first anniversary'.

December: We spend our autumn driving to and around Turkey. After several rainless weeks overseas, my December diary records a trot round Daeda's Wood in a steady drizzle: '… the sheer smell of life – 2004's in gentle decay but plenty of promise for 2005 … a wren rummaging in a pile of dead leaves, amazingly a scattering of yarrow still in flower… . And at this time you can see the bare bones of the trees.' Euphoria.

The Druid Wedding

Daeda's Visitors

Over the years, visitors to the wood and to our displays have made kind comments. Here are some of them

This is a great idea. The people of Deddington are fortunate indeed to be part of such an enterprise.

P Chard

A very informative and interesting project which will be of benefit for many generations to come both for Deddington and peripheral parishes.

B.G.Lane

Most impressed with the work done and the imagination used

Pamela Brownlie

We love to walk from Deddington through the fields to the woods. The prize for our Labrador, Gracie, is that she can leap straight into the river for a swim when we get there ...

Sally and Colin Lambert, Deddington

Jean and Douglas Ward lived in Deddington for many years, running a B&B at Maunds Farmhouse. They both taught locally, and, as Miss Austin, Jean was Senior Mistress at the Windmill School from 1959 to 1970. Both sang in the Parish Church choir from 1969 to 1988. I had known Jean for over 40 years and after her death in 1999, although Daeda's Wood had been removed from the planting list, I asked the Woodland Trust (having been a member for many years) if, in view of Jean's special connection with Deddington, I could have a tree dedicated to her in Daeda's Wood. It was agreed, so I feel especially fond of Daeda's Wood. (I had previously had four trees in the wood dedicated to friends from Aynho.)

Margaret Arnold, Deddington

DAEDA'S VISITORS

Sunday 24 November 1996 was a surreal day. It was one of those raw November days when the only thing to do was curl up by a log fire with the Sunday papers. But not this day. My sister had died of cancer the previous week and the funeral was fixed for the following day. With mixed emotions sculling around, a symbol of stability and continuity was needed. I decided to plant a tree for Helen. So, despite a raging high temperature, I dragged my husband and two sons off to Daeda's Wood. We did plant a couple of trees, with much laughter and larking around, before I was whisked off home for a hot toddy. I don't know which trees they were, and it doesn't really matter – Helen is out there somewhere!

Mary Robinson, Deddington

I have known Daeda's Wood since it was a bare field, through the tree planting stage up until today. It has given my little dog and myself many hours of pleasure, walking and watching it grow and develop in all the various seasons, along with the wild flower meadow and the various birds and wild life. Thank you to everyone involved.

Helen Hunter, Banbury

Looking baack at it, its rely niec
Rosie

Coming down to Daeda's Wood on a bright day of the dying summer, I found a promise of glorious days to come. This was my first visit but not my last as I hope to watch, in the company of grandchildren, the evolution of the wood's ecological system. Please plant a further scattering of benches!

K.R.Dickson, Deddington

An enchanting wood that manages to be both restful and stimulating. A green haven. A site for sore eyes. Truly a wood for all seasons.

Norman Stone, Deddington

Of all the projects mooted for the millennium, few can have involved less hype and left a more lasting legacy than the Woodland Trust's Woods on your Doorstep project. When I first heard that the Trust were looking to buy the plot by Bloxham Bridge, it seemed to us a most worthwhile project to support – and it has not been a disappointment. It has been a delight to watch it grow and to think that on our doorstep we have this permanent growing asset.

Colin Cohen, Barford St Michael

2005

***S**pring-Summer:* Daeda has a shaggy sort of year. Although the creeping thistle is retreating from under the canopy, in one or two open areas it has grown to the height of saplings, much to the delight of the butterflies (p.30). Sadly, the wild flowers seem to have retreated, too. In some areas they seem to be fighting a losing battle with a particularly sturdy species of grasses. No need to panic, we are told. This could be cyclical or reflect the health of the environment at a given moment. Time will tell.

In May, our primary school PTA organise a fund-raising walk, which attracts 222 entrants and features Daeda's Wood, where the children make brass rubbings of animal prints. A tidy sum is raised and there are even more ambitious plans for 2006.

In July we organise a village walk. It is rather poorly attended but most of the Friends join in and we enjoy the accompanying wine and nibbles.

The Environment Agency arrive to do some drastic pollarding, leaving piles of brushwood and stacks of logs all along the Swere's bank. Presumably there will be more sunlight on the water and the damselflies will approve.

September: An email comes from a Friend, Colin Cohen. 'This will mystify you', it reads, giving an extremely long web address. I remain mystified for some weeks until another friend explains about gps (geo positioning systems) and geocaching (pronounced geocashing). This is a kind of treasure hunt on a global scale involving nearly a quarter of a million sites in over 200 countries and, incredibly, one is in Daeda's Wood.

It is not so much a treasure hunt as a challenge in orienteering for solo, group or family outings. The cache usually yields a collection of modest items from which you may take one providing you replace it with another. More to the point for most geocachers is the log book in which to enter your name before heading for the website («http://www.geocaching.com/seek/cache_details.aspx?guid=6cff00f7-512f-46ea186-a746e230e4f4») to record your success with appropriate comment.

New Year's Day 2006: Happy Birthday, Daeda. A lot of people are about, enjoying a wood that was once a barley field.

Jill Butler finds the wood has grown

Early spring walkers

Frost on pollarded logs

Daeda's Future

Ten years is a short lifespan for a woodland and 'perpetuity', the time we expect the woodland to remain, is even more difficult to perceive.

The planting here has created a belt of important riverside woodland. It is a mix of trees and shrubs, typical of flood plain and wet woodland. As the interest in this woodland is leaning hard towards being a conservation wet woodland, this will lead to any work within it being very low key.

Coppicing and widening along the ride edges and keeping the meadow cut and raked will maintain the growth of the osiers and ensure that the paths remain open and sunny, becoming a haven for butterflies and other invertebrates. Keeping an open feel to the woodland will also ensure that established views are maintained. Obviously there will be some thinning of the wood. Some of the cut trees should be left to increase the dead wood habitat. If there are any budding basket-makers locally, they may be able to use the osiers that are coppiced. The available markets will be explored when the opportunity arises.

Maintaining the stream edge pollards will increase the interest for invertebrates and secure the future of these large trees for many years to come. This will also ensure that the river edge does not become shaded and that the damselflies and other sun-loving invertebrates continue to flourish. One day an otter family may establish itself in the otter holt.

Low impact management in this exciting small woodland will create a robust area for conservation in the future. Imagine if you can Daeda's Wood in 75 years' time with the open paths amongst 70–80 feet tall oaks and ashes with an understorey of osier, haw-thorn, blackthorn and Guelder rose. There will be bramble and, after the winter floods, several wet spots. Several of the large trees will have fallen and as they rot will have been colonised by fungi and be full of beetles. Imagine the small birds that hunt through the trees and make the bushes burst with life as you wander through. Imagine!

JOHN BROWN
Senior Woodland Officer

You can follow the wood's development in the *Deddington News*, or by going to «www.deddington.org.uk/community/daedaswood.html».

DAEDA'S TREES

Ash	*Fraxinus excelsior*	1485
Crack willow	*Salix fragilis*	200
Pendunculate oak	*Quercus robur*	840
Almond willow	*Salix triandra*	120
White willow	*Salix alba*	120
Goat willow	*Salix caprea*	120
Grey poplar	*Populus canescens*	210
Alder	*Alnus glutinosa*	130
Osier	*Salix viminalis*	130
Purple willow	*Salix purpurea*	85
Black poplar	*Populus nigra*	15
Aspen	*Populus tremula*	15
Common hawthorn	*Crataegus monogyna*	85
Blackthorn	*Prunus spinosa*	85
Guelder rose	*Viburnum opulus*	40

(Source: Woodland Trust)

DAEDA'S WOOD FLORA LIST

Angelica, wild, *Angelica sylvestris*
Arrowhead (aquatic), *Sagittaria sagittifolia*
Bedstraw, hedge, *Galium mollugo*
Bellflower, nettle-leaved, *Campanula trachelium*
Bindweed, hedge, *Calystegia sepium*
Bistort, *Persicaria bistorta*
Buttercup, creeping, *Ranunculus repens*
Buttercup, meadow, *Ranunculus acris*
Campion, bladder, *Silene vulgaris*
Campion, white, *Silene latifolia*
Campion, red, *Silene dioica*
Celandine, lesser, *Ranunculus ficaria*
Cleavers, *Galium aparine*
Clover, white, *Trifolium repens*
Clover, red, *Trifolium pratense*
Cow parsley, *Anthriscus sylvestris*
Cowslip, *Primula veris*
Cranesbill, meadow, *Geranium pratense*
Cuckoo flower, *Cardamine pratensis*
Daisy, ox-eye, *Leucanthemum vulgare*
Deadnettle, white, *Lamium album*
Deadnettle, red, *Lamium purpureum*
Dock, broad-leaved, *Rumex obtusifolius*
Field scabious, *Knautia arvensis*
Forgetmenot, field, *Myosotis arvensis*
Hempnettle, common, *Galeopsis tetrahit*
Herb Robert, *Geraniunm robertianum*
Knapweed, common, *Centaurea nigra*
Mallow, musk, *Malva moschata*
Meadowsweet, *Filipendula ulmaria*

Mousear, common, *Cerastuim fontanum*
Nettle, common, *Urtica dioica*
Nightshade, woody, *Solanum dulcamara*
Nipplewort, *Lapsana communis*
Pansy, wild, *Viola tricolor*
Plantain, greater, *Plantago major*
Plantain, ribwort, *Plantago lanceolata*
Poppy, common, *Papaver rhoeas*
Primrose, *Primula vulgaris*
Ragged robin, *Lychnis flos-cuculi*
Redshank, *Persicaria maculosa*
St John's Wort, hairy, *Hypericum hirsutum*
Self-heal, *Prunella vulgaris*
Sorrel, common, *Rumex acetosa*
Sow-thistle, prickly, *Sonchus asper*
Teasel, *Dipsacus fullonum*
Thistle, creeping, *Cirsium arvense*
Thistle, marsh, *Cirsium palustre*
Trefoil, hop, *Trifolium campestre*
Vetch, tufted, *Vicia cracca*
Vetchling, meadow, *Lathyrus pratensis*
Violet, white, *Viola alba*
Water-lily (aquatic), *Nuphar lutea*
Willowherb, greater, *Epilobium hirsutum*
Yarrow, *Achillea millefolium*
Garden escapees:
  Comfrey   Purple crocus
  Daffodil   Snowdrop

(Compiled 2002–05)

Woods on your Doorstep

200 Woods for 2000

The Woodland Trust was created in 1972 with the commitments to:
- no further loss of ancient woodland
- restoring and improving the biodiversity of woods
- increasing new native woodland
- increasing people's awareness and enjoyment of woodland

With the last two of these aims particularly in mind, in November 1995 the Trust launched its Woods on Your Doorstep project to create 200 new community woods close to cities, towns and villages in England and Wales for the Millennium. The following year the scheme was expanded to include 50 woods in Northern Ireland, the whole project backed by £10.5 million from the Millennium Commission.

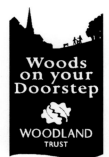

In most cases, local communities were asked to raise a substantial contribution to 'their' wood, thus showing their commitment to its future. This has often also had the benefit of triggering the formation of a local support group, such as the Friends of Daeda's Wood.

Five years after the project was launched, its success was celebrated at a House of Commons reception hosted by the MP for that rather more established wood, Sherwood Forest.

Indeed, the original aim was exceeded by 8 per cent, the final total of newly created woodland covering 810 hectares (2.174 acres), with one and a half million trees planted on roughly the equivalent of 2,100 football pitches. It has also included the creation of ponds, marshes, meadows and hedgerows.

Local communities were given the opportunity in each case to discuss the nature of the wood, its name and any special features they would like included.

The first of all to be completed was Daeda's Wood.

200 Sites

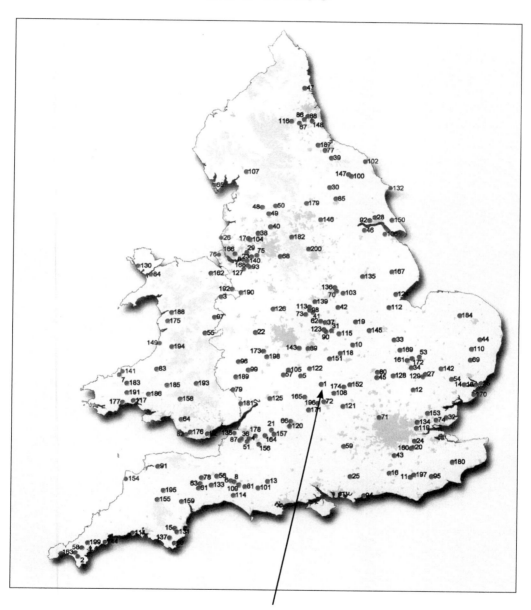

No. 1, Daeda's Wood, Oxfordshire

Acknowledgements

Commissioning editor	Kristin Thompson
Imaging	Colin Robinson

Text
Annual diaries — Sylvie Nickels
Other text — As attributed

Photographs — *Cover: top*, George Spenceley; *bottom*, Colin Robinson
Pages 13, 16, 17, 33: Peter Sheasby
Other pages: Sylvie Nickels, Colin Robinson
George Spenceley

Illustrations — *Page 1:* Maps and Access: by kind permission of
Deddington Map Group
Pages 8–9: Vivien Wilson for the Woodland Trust
Page 22: by kind permission of Cherwell District Council
Pages 2, 23, 40, 43: by kind permission of the
Woodland Trust

The Friends of Daeda's Wood gratefully acknowledge financial assistance from the Woodland Trust.

FRIENDS OF DAEDA'S WOOD
Present and Past

Chairman	Sylvie Nickels
Secretary	Yvonne Twomey
Treasurer	Chris Twomey

Colin Cohen, Sue Goddard, Walter Meagher, John Neild, Molly Neild,
Colin Robinson, Kristin Thompson, Nancy White, Jackie Williamson,
Mike Williamson